VISION BOARD

Clipart BOOK

By: DestinyManieste Books

Create vision boards from 100s of
images, related to finances, health, love, beauty & more, to
design a life that you love!

WHAT IS A VISION BOARD?

A vision board is a sacred creation. It is a physical representation of your dreams, aspirations and goals in the form of a collage created and designed entirely by you. This collage often includes photos, magazine cut-outs, keepsakes and quotes—anything that will help you to clearly visualize exactly what you want in your life.

A vision board serves as a source of inspiration and motivation, all the while keeping you focused on what it is you want to achieve, and what actions you must take to manifest your dreams into your reality.

This board is meant to be placed somewhere you can see it daily, ideally in the hours just before sleep, or just after waking, when it is easiest to program your subconscious mind. (Your bedroom wall, an alter, etc.)

WHY DO I NEED A VISION BOARD?

In this world, you are bombarded with images, ideas and programming that don't come from within. You are constantly being fed messages and images that sink into your vulnerable subconsciousness and often work negatively against you. This, combined with a daily routine of being overworked, stressed and feeling trapped in your own life make for a dangerous concoction—one that kills dreams, and passion.

Considering that the media keeps you focused on the negativity in the world, distracted with celebrities with whom you don't to relate, and demotivated by discouraging statistics that make you wonder if it even makes sense to work towards your dreams, you can see how external factors seriously effect your drive, distract you from your own goals, and keep you living a less than ideal life.

It is a fact that what you focus on expands, thus it is imperative that you concentrate on the right things.

A vision board is a reminder that your life is completely yours to design, and that you can indeed have anything you desire. It provides a clear image of what you want, and keeps your thoughts in alignment with your goals to inspire you to take meaningful actions everyday to achieve them, as well as attract what you want to you.

A vision board is also a reminder that you yourself, like a canvas, can be transformed into personal masterpiece of your very own making. If you want to be more assertive, well-read and well-spoken, worldly, creative, even if you just want a better beach body, these are all achievable when you make yourself and your personal goals a top priority.

Your vision board conveys the message that the end of the day, you are in control. Everything you decide to direct your energies towards and each action you take each day, is shaping your future.

A vision board is meant to pull you out of negative repetitive programmed thinking, and have you align your thought patterns and actions with the outcomes that you want.

Remember, your goals can be big or small, and of any nature you desire. There is no right or wrong when it comes to your own personal vision for yourself and your life.

WILL A VISION BOARD WORK FOR ME?

Vision boards work on the basis of visualization and the law of attraction. This law teaches that whatever you direct your energies and attention on is what you will see more of.

Example: If a basketball player constantly thinks about not wanting to miss their shots, they may actually end up performing poorly during a game because their focus was 'missing the shot'.

But, if the same basketball player visualizes successfully making all of their shots, they will likely actually re-create this success in their reality.

A study by Psychology Today compared people who went to the gym regularly to those who visualized themselves doing workouts in their heads. The findings were very interesting. Those who went to the gym increased their muscle mass by 30%, and those who did the mental exercises increased their muscle mass by 13.5%. There is a powerful correlation between one's visualization and physical results.

A vision board is meant to help you to put visualization to work and attach strong emotions of gratitude for what it is that you want. (This is key, strong feelings of wanting, only begets more 'want'. Be grateful for what you are working towards, as though you already have it. The universe responds powerfully to gratitude.)

Of course, when it comes to your goals, you must be willing to also put in the effort otherwise you may end up feeling disappointed. Important as it is, visualization is only the first step. Be sure to couple it with work and dedication to bring your vision into your reality.

As you begin to achieve your goals and milestones, be sure to revisit your vision board and change things up every so often, to reflect current goals.

HOW DO I MAKE A VISION BOARD?

Making a vision board is quite simple, even without crafting and design experience.

You will need:

- Some kind of board, like a poster board, cork board, pin board etc.
- A pair of scissors to cut out images, and words like those provided in this book.
- Tape, pins or glue.
- You can also use other optional materials such as markers, stickers, or other embellishments—so long as they make you feel inspired.
- You will also need time. The process of creating a vision board is not something to be rushed. Take some time for yourself to really contemplate how you would like your life to look. Turn off all distractions, and set the mood. You can play some inspiring music, light candles, or burn some incense. The point is to create an atmosphere where you can freely create.

Above is just a short and general list of things you will need to get your vision board started, but remember, you can put just about anything you want on it—so don't let this list restrict you. If you want to put a spritz of your favorite cologne or perfume, or glue seashells or feathers to your board, then feel free.

When it comes to choosing your quotes and images, you should choose the ones that truly resonate with you, and properly reflect and convey your vision for your future.

When you decide on the images and quotes you want to use, keep in mind that there is no wrong way to position them. Do what is most natural to you. You can create a collage by placing each image wherever feels right, or you can take a more organized approach and divide your board up by sections. (Ex. Health, Finances and Relationships). You can even have separate boards for different goals.

So what are you waiting for? The life of your dreams starts here. Make yourself into your own personal project, start envisioning exactly what you want your future to look like and actively working towards the manifestation of your dreams and actualization of your goals by making mindful decisions guided by your own sacred vision.

Today is a brand new day. It is a blank canvas, and ready to be filled with your vision. This is the beginning of the rest of your life, how you shape it is entirely up to you.

I AM HANDSOME.

I AM A CREATOR

I AM Healthy
I AM Healed
I AM Whole

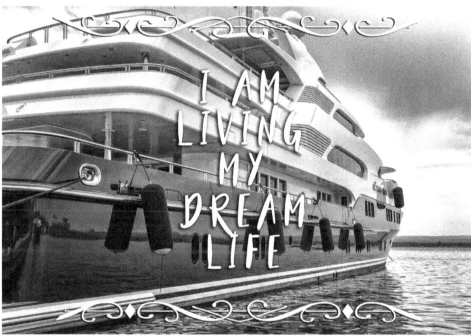

I AM LIVING MY DREAM LIFE

VOLUNTEER

I am HEALTHY

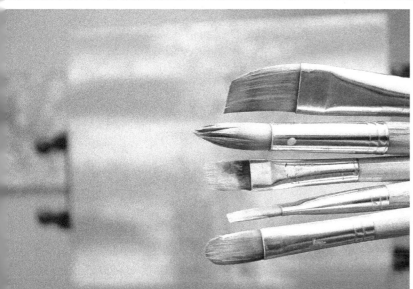

Draw
EVERYDAY

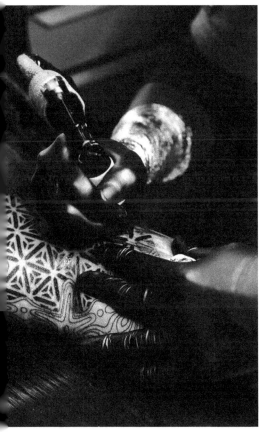

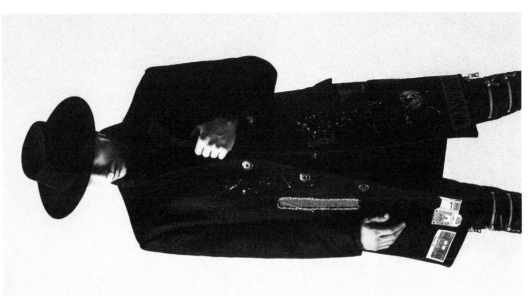

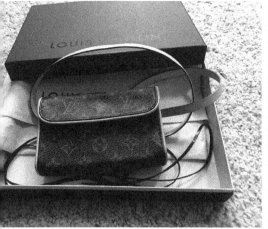

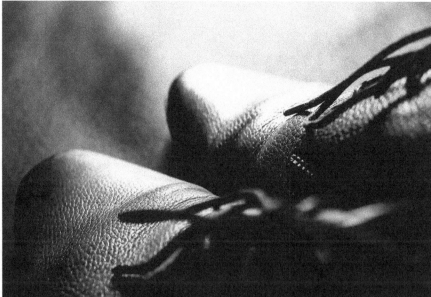

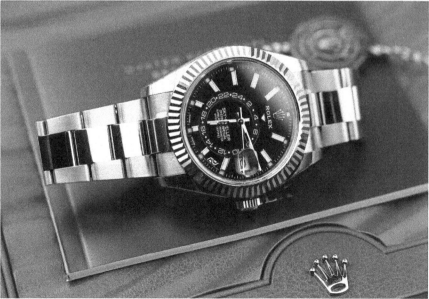

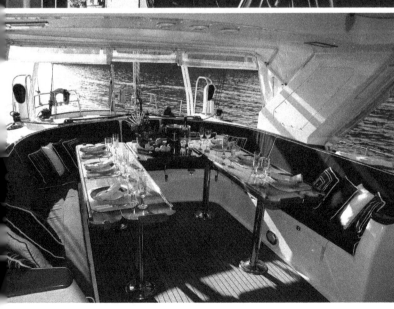
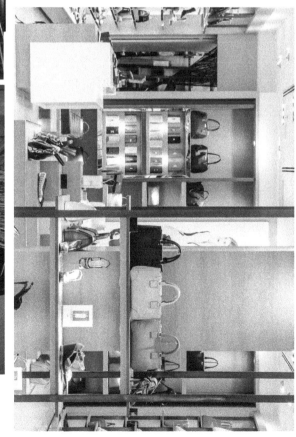

Forbes

I DON'T CHASE RECOGNITION OR FAME.

I FOLLOW MY PASSIONS AND PURPOSE,

AND BY DOING SO,

WEALTH,

Fame & Recognition

CHASE ME.

I will Tell My Story

"There's no greater agony than bearing a n untold story inside of you."
- Maya Angelou

BRAZIL

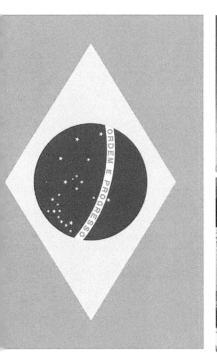

斜日掩蓮塘幾回審撲紅衫覺是
胡山唱過客

乙酉槏剥胡荷軒製

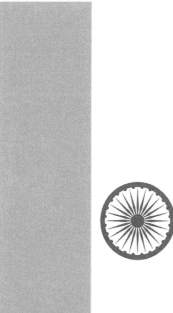

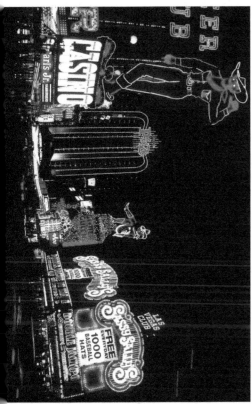

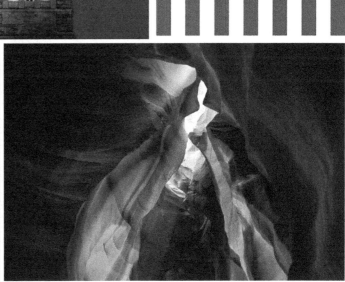

CPSIA information can be obtained
at www.ICGtesting.com
Printed in the USA
LVHW060953100621
689898LV00008B/68

9 781777 643249